Edmund Janes James

**Education of Business Men**

Edmund Janes James

**Education of Business Men**

ISBN/EAN: 9783337215538

Printed in Europe, USA, Canada, Australia, Japan

Cover: Foto ©Andreas Hilbeck / pixelio.de

More available books at **www.hansebooks.com**

# EDUCATION OF BUSINESS MEN.

## AN ADDRESS

BEFORE THE CONVENTION

OF THE

# American Bankers' Association

At Saratoga, September 3, 1890,

BY

## EDMUND J. JAMES, Ph. D.,

*Professor of Public Finance and Administration in the Wharton School of Finance*

*and Economy of the University of Pennsylvania,*

*Philadelphia.*

PLAN OF THE

WHARTON SCHOOL OF FINANCE AND ECONOMY.

PROCEEDINGS OF THE ASSOCIATION RELATIVE TO THE ADDRESS
OF PROFESSOR JAMES, AND UPON THE FOUNDING
OF SCHOOLS OF FINANCE AND ECONOMY.

PUBLISHED BY

WILLIAM B. GREENE, SECRETARY,

NEW YORK.

1891.

# COMMITTEE ON SCHOOLS OF FINANCE AND ECONOMY

OF

EXECUTIVE COUNCIL,

# AMERICAN BANKERS' ASSOCIATION.

---

---

# Officers

# AMERICAN BANKERS' ASSOCIATION

*September, 1890.*

---

### PRESIDENT.
MORTON McMICHAEL,
Cashier First National Bank, Philadelphia, Penn.

### FIRST VICE-PRESIDENT.
RICHARD M. NELSON,
President Commercial Bank, Selma, Ala.

### TREASURER.
GEORGE F. BAKER.
President First National Bank, New York City.

### SECRETARY.
WILLIAM B. GREENE.
128 Broadway, New York.

---

## Executive Council.

*(For term of two years.)*

JOHN JAY KNOX, Chairman,
President National Bank of the Republic, New York City.

WILLIAM H. RHAWN,
President National Bank of the Republic, Philadelphia, Penn.

ASA P. POTTER,
President Maverick National Bank, Boston, Mass.

LYMAN J. GAGE,
Vice-President First National Bank, Chicago, Ill.

A. U. WYMAN,
President Omaha Loan and Trust Company, Omaha, Neb.

EMORY WENDELL,
President First National Bank, Detroit, Mich.

S. A. HARRIS,
President Northwestern National Bank, Minneapolis, Minn.

*(For the term of one year.)*

WILLIAM P. ST. JOHN,
President Mercantile National Bank, New York City.

J. J. P. ODELL,
President Union National Bank, Chicago, Ill.

LOGAN H. ROOTS,
President Arkansas Loan and Trust Company, Little Rock, Ark.

JOSEPH S. CHICK,
President National Bank of Kansas City, Kansas City, Mo.

CHARLES MERIWETHER,
Assistant Cashier Falls City Bank, Louisville, Ky.

M. M. WHITE,
President Fourth National Bank, Cincinnati, Ohio.

S. G. MURPHY,
President First National Bank, San Francisco, Cal.

*(For the term of three years.)*

GEORGE S. COE,
President American Exchange National Bank, New York City.

EDWARD B. JUDSON,
President First National Bank, Syracuse, N. Y.

CHARLES PARSONS,
President State Bank, St. Louis, Mo.

EDWARD S. BUTTS,
President Vicksburg Bank, Vicksburg, Miss.

GEORGE A. BUTLER,
President National Tradesmen's Bank, New Haven, Conn.

JAMES H. WILLOCK,
President Second National Bank, Pittsburgh, Pa.

JESSE G. HAMMER,
Cashier Union National Bank, Atlantic City, N. J.

---

## Vice Presidents.

### Alabama.
JOSEPH F. JOHNSTON, President Alabama National Bank, Birmingham.

### Arizona.
M. W. KALES, President National Bank of Arixona, Phœnix.

### Arkansas.
CREED T. WALKER, Cashier Bank of Little Rock, Little Rock.

### California.
E. F. SPENCE, President First National Bank, Los Angeles.

### Colorado.
E. L. RAYMOND, Vice-President State National Bank, Denver.

### Connecticut.
JAMES B. POWELL, President Mercantile National Bank, Hartford.

### Delaware.
EDWARD BETTS, President First National Bank, Wilmington.

### District of Columbia.
E. FRANCIS RIGGS, Riggs & Co., Bankers, Washington,

### Florida.
D. G. AMBLER, President National Bank of State of Florida, Jacksonville.

### Georgia.
A. W. HILL, Vice-President Gate City National Bank, Atlanta.

### Idaho.
A. G. REDWAY, Cashier First National Bank of Idaho, Boise City.

### Illinois.
JOHN C. NEELY, Cashier Merchants' National Bank, Chicago.

### Indiana.
VOLNEY T. MALOTT, President of the Indiana National Bank, Indianapolis.

### Iowa.
JUSTUS CLARK, President Red Oak National Bank, Red Oak.

### Kansas.
GEORGE B. LORD, President Johnson County Bank, Olathe.

### Kentucky.
PHIL. T. WATKINS, Cashier First National Bank, Owensboro.

### Louisiana.
THOMAS R. ROACH, Cashier Southern National Bank, New Orleans.

### Maine.
STEPHEN R. SMALL, President Casco National Bank, Portland.

### Maryland.
E. J. PENNIMAN, Cashier First National Bank, Baltimore.

### Massachusetts.
ISAAC T. BURR, President National Bank North America, Boston.

### Michigan.
F. W. HAYES, Vice-President Preston National Bank, Detroit.

### Minnesota.
HENRY P. UPHAM, President First National Bank, St. Paul.

### Mississippi.
LEE RICHARDSON, President Delta Trust and Banking Co., Vicksburg.

### Missouri.
C. J. WHITE, Cashier National Bank of Commerce, Kansas City.

### Montana.
SAMUEL T. HAUSER, President First National Bank, Helena.

### Nebraska.
HENRY W. YATES, President Nebraska National Bank, Omaha.

### Nevada.
D. A. BENLER, President First National Bank, Reno.

### New Hampshire.
GEORGE B. CHANDLER, Cashier Amoskeag National Bank, Manchester.

### New Jersey.
CHARLES S. GRAHAM, President North Ward National Bank, Newark.

### New Mexico.
JEFFERSON RAYNOLDS, President First National Bank, Las Vegas.

### New York.
G. A. VAN ALLEN, President First National Bank, Albany.

### North Carolina.
W. E. BREESE, President First National Bank, Asheville.

### North Dakota.
E. ASHLEY MEARS, President Mortgage Bank and Investment Co., Fargo.

### Ohio.
CHARLES A. STEVENS, Assistant Cashier Merchants' National Bank, Cincinnati.

### Oklahoma.
J. W. McNEAL, President Guthrie National Bank, Guthrie.

### Oregon.
R. L. DURHAM, Cashier Commercial National Bank, Portland.

### Pennsylvania.
WILLIAM H. PECK, Cashier Third National Bank, Scranton.

### Rhode Island.
WM. H. PARK, Cashier First National Bank, Pawtucket.

### South Carolina.
ANDREW SIMONDS, President First National Bank, Charleston.

### South Dakota.
JOHN D. LAWLER, President First National Bank, Mitchell.

### Tennessee.
R. DUDLEY FRAYSER, President Memphis City Bank, Memphis.

### Texas.
EUGENE SIBLEY, Vice-President First National Bank, Victoria.

### Utah.
L. S. HILLS, Cashier Deseret National Bank, Salt Lake City.

### Vermont.
CHAS. W. MUSSEY, Cashier Merchants' National Bank of Rutland.

### Virginia.
J. W. LOCKWOOD, Cashier National Bank of Virginia, Richmond.

### Washington.
W. J. THOMPSON, President Merchants' National Bank, Tacoma.

### West Virginia.
F. P. JEPSON, Cashier Bank of the Ohio Valley, Wheeling.

### Wisconsin.
N. B. VAN SLYKE, President First National Bank, Madison.

### Wyoming.
HENRY G. HAY, Cashier Stockgrowers' National Bank, Cheyenne.

# AMERICAN BANKERS' ASSOCIATION.

## COMMITTEE ON SCHOOLS OF FINANCE AND ECONOMY.

*January 1, 1891.*

At a meeting of the Executive Council of the American Bankers' Association, held in New York City on October 16, 1889, the following resolution, offered by Mr. William H. Rhawn, was unanimously adopted:

"*Resolved*, That a committee of not less than three or more than five be appointed by the chairman, to whom shall be submitted the subject of the preparation or procurement of a paper to be read at the next Convention of the Association, upon the establishment of schools in connection with the universities and colleges of the country, of general scope and character like that of 'The Wharton School of Finance and Economy,' connected with the University of Pennsylvania; and the best means by which the establishment and endowment of such schools may be promoted and fostered by the Association."

The Chairman, Hon. John Jay Knox, appointed as a Committee under the resolution, Mr. William H. Rhawn, Mr. Logan C. Murray, and Mr. Morton McMichael.

The Committee invited Edmund J. James, Ph. D., Professor of Public Finance and Administration in the Wharton School of Finance and Economy of the University of Pennsylvania, Philadelphia, to prepare and read the proposed paper upon Schools of Finance and Economy before the next Convention, which invitation he kindly accepted.

In announcing the forthcoming paper by Professor James, the Committee presented the general plan of the Wharton School, with an introductory statement by its beneficent founder, Mr. Joseph Wharton, and invited expressions of opinion upon the subject from bankers and others, in response to which numerous letters strongly commending the establishment of such schools were received.

Professor James prepared and delivered an instructive and scholarly address before the Association, at the Convention at Saratoga, on September 3, 1890, and the Convention unanimously voted him the thanks of the Association for his address, and ordered that it should be published with the proceedings, and also in separate pamphlet form, together with the plan of the Wharton School.

Resolutions relative to the address and to the establishment of Schools of Finance and Economy were submitted to the Convention and after discussion referred to the Executive Council, which reported back the following resolutions, which were unanimously adopted by the Convention:

"*Resolved*, That the American Bankers' Association most earnestly commends, not only to the bankers, but to all intelligent and progressive citizens throughout the country, the founding of Schools of Finance and

Economy, for the business training of youth, to be established in connection with the universities and colleges of the land, upon a general plan like that of the Wharton School of Finance and Economy of the University of Pennsylvania, so ably set forth by Professor James in his most admirable address before this Convention :

" *Resolved*, That the Executive Council is hereby directed to carefully consider and, if possible, devise some feasible plan whereby this Association may encourage or promote the organization of a School or of Schools of Finance and Economy among our institutions of learning, and report upon the same to the next Convention."

At a meeting of the Executive Council, held at the close of the Convention on September 5, the foregoing resolutions were referred to the undersigned Committee, appointed under the direction of the Council by Mr. Charles Parsons, Chairman pro tem, as a Committee on Schools of Finance and Economy.

In accordance with the several resolutions of the Convention and of the Executive Council, the Committee here present the Address of Professor James and the Plan of the Wharton School, together with the proceedings of the Convention relating thereto, to which the thoughtful and serious consideration of bankers and all others interested in the problem of the best education for the coming business men of the country, is earnestly invited.

Before entering fully upon the consideration of a feasible plan whereby the American Bankers' Association may encourage or promote the organization of a great educational institution for the training of youth into business men, such as has been so vividly portrayed by Professor James, and of Schools of Finance and Economy in connection with the universities and colleges of the land, the Committee desires to receive and respectfully invites, from the members of the Association and bankers generally, and from all friends of the cause of such education, expressions of opinion and suggestions which may aid the Committee in its work, to be addressed to the Chairman or any of its members, and for which the thanks of the Committee are here tendered in advance.

WILLIAM H. RHAWN,
GEORGE S. COE,
LYMAN J. GAGE,
MORTON MCMICHAEL,
ASA P. POTTER.

# SCHOOLS OF FINANCE AND ECONOMY
## ADDRESS OF PROFESSOR EDMUND J. JAMES, PH.D.

*Professor of Public Finances and Administration, Wharton School of Finance and Economy, University of Pennsylvania—before Convention of American Bankers' Association, Saratoga, N. Y., Sept. 3, 1890.*

MEMBERS OF THE AMERICAN BANKERS' ASSOCIATION:

Your committee have done me the honor of inviting me to address you upon the subject of Schools of Finance and Economy. I respond to this invitation with much pleasure. It is a delight to speak to an intelligent audience upon a question of general interest. It is a source of special pleasure to present the claims of an important subject to a set of men who have unusual means of influencing public opinion in regard to it.

There are few subjects of more general interest to an American audience than those relating to education. Just at present, moreover, the questions pertaining to higher education are receiving an unusual share of attention. The enormous expansion in our scheme of higher instruction which has taken place in the last twenty years, and which has revolutionized all our leading institutions, has brought to the front a number of fundamental questions which have not yet been fully answered.

Under the American political and social system the hope of general and rapid progress in any line lies chiefly in interesting the public at large in the matter. It is not possible with us, if an improvement is to be made in our college system, for example, to present the matter to a Minister of Education who, upon being convinced of the wisdom of a proposed change, may, by a simple order, revolutionize every college in the country. We must, on the contrary, try to reach the public and create a demand for the change; or persuade the leading college presidents or leading trustees of our great institutions to try the experiment.

I count myself happy, therefore, that I have an opportunity to present the subject of this paper to your Association. You are the very people who should be interested in it for its own sake, and whose co-operation would ensure its promotion. Many of you, moreover, are trustees of colleges and universities and from such positions have unusual opportunities to affect the educational policy of the country. I am addressing, therefore, not merely American citizens who may be presumed to have an interest in education for its own sake; not merely American business men who should have a very special interest in all that relates to business education, but also in many cases trustees of our higher institutions of learning whose solemn duty it is to seek out and try all things which may help in the advancement of our higher instruction.

The subject of my paper is the higher education of the future business man or, as it may be otherwise stated, a college course for the future business man; for this is the purpose of the Schools of Finance and Economy mentioned in the title of the paper. I do not know how I can present the subject to your consideration better than to give you some account of the experiment we are trying in Philadelphia in the Wharton School of Finance and Economy, a sub-department of the University of Pennsylvania. I do this the more readily, as it was the success of this school which first attracted the attention of your Committee to the sub-

ject, and it was my connection with the school which led them to invite me
to deliver this address.

You have all doubtless received a communication, sent out by your Committee on the 15th of November last, relating to the Wharton School of
Finance and Economy. Appended to the communication was a copy of
the original plan or prospectus of the school, drawn up by Mr. Joseph
Wharton and submitted to the Board of Trustees of the University of Pennsylvania as an indication of what he wished the school to be, whose establishment he secured by the gift of $100,000 to the University. In that pros-
pectus and in an address recently delivered before the Wharton School
Alumni Association,* Mr. Wharton indicates the reasons which led him to
establish this school. As they were reasons which go to the very root of the
matter, and involve some of the most important aspects of our whole system of higher education, I cannot do better than present the subject along
the lines there laid down. His discussion of the subject, though brief, is
direct and convincing. It involves three points : the inadequacy of existing
facilities for the higher education of our business classes ; the desirability
of having such facilities ; suggestions as to what can and should be done.

An American youth who is looking forward to a business career and has
completed the ordinary grammar school course, stands face to face with an
interesting and important problem. Shall I seek a situation in some business
house, closing my school education with what I have now, and trusting to the
friction of active life for further education, or shall I go to some other
school a while longer, and trust to the benefits of the training there to make
up for the greater practical knowledge which I might get in the same
number of years in the counting house, factory or bank ? The average boy
in our American life decides in favor of going into business at once. This
may be explained, of course, on the ground that the average boy has no
money with which to pay his way at higher schools. But even the average
boy whose parents can afford to send him longer to school makes the same
choice ; nay, the average son of well-to-do or wealthy parents does the same
thing. Now why is this ? Why do such a large number of those able to
get this higher training turn aside and refuse it ? The old answer was that
they are too ignorant or lazy or indifferent. Neither they nor their parents
have any notion of the immense advantage they would derive from this
higher training. There is doubtless much truth in this reply ; but, perhaps,
it is also true that this so-called higher education appears to bear but little
relation to their future work. It may all be very nice. It may belong to
the accomplishments of life. It makes doubtless a fine dessert ; but it is in
all probability a pure article of luxury which no energetic and vigorous
person who is determined to succeed in the fierce conflict of competitive
business can afford to acquire at the cost of years of effort. This is doubtless a very material, but also a very natural way of viewing the problem.

Now, what courses are open to the youth who determines to get something more in the way of an education before going into business? He might
take a medical or theological course ; the former would increase his knowl-

---

* " Is a College Education Advantageous to a Business Man ? " Address delivered before the
Wharton School Association at its third annual reception, February 20, 1890, at the Manufacturers'
Club, Philadelphia.

edge of facts enormously, the latter would sharpen his logical acumen. Such a proposition, however, would seem absurd, and very few students would ever think of adopting this plan. The youth might take a law school course ; he would find much in that work to quicken his faculties and some information that would be of practical value to him in his business. But still, if this were the only opportunity for higher education it is safe to say that but few youths looking forward to a business career would ever get this higher training. We have now also the technical schools. Our youth might graduate in civil or mining engineering, architecture, etc., etc. In each of these and similar courses he would find something of value. But the same thing applies to them as to medicine and theology ; but few students would ever take these courses unless they intended to follow the corresponding profession. What then remains? Only the so-called Commercial or Business College and the literary college. It is safe to say then as our educational conditions lie, that the only opportunity for higher education now open to youths looking forward to a business career is to be found in one of these institutions.

As to the so-called Commercial or Business Colleges, I would not willingly do them an injustice. I believe that they are a great and permanent constituent of our educational system. They have done and are doing and are destined to continue doing, a great and useful work. But the training which they, with few exceptions, furnish can scarcely be called a higher training at all. It has to do with "facilities"—indeed chiefly with manual facilities—writing, reckoning, etc., those things that go to make up a good clerk, things of great value in themselves, things which every business man would be the better for having, and yet things which after all are only facilities ; they do not touch the essence of successful business management or tend to develop the higher sides of business activity ; they bear little or no relation to those broader views characteristic of the business manager as distinct from the business clerk and are of course next to useless as a means of liberal education. The knowledge which they impart, however valuable in itself, "does not suffice to fit a young man for the struggle of commercial life, for wise management of a private estate or for efficient public service."*

Our literary colleges, on the other hand, are, though in quite a different way, also incapable of answering this demand for the higher education and training of the business man. The average curriculum of the American college is made up chiefly of Latin, Greek, and higher mathematics with a dab of natural science, modern languages and history. I would not by any means underestimate the value of such training viewed from a subjective standpoint. A vigorous training in the classics and higher mathematics undoubtedly sharpens a man's intellectual faculties ; it trains his tastes and widens his whole mental horizon ; but it also, as things go now, and as they probably will go for all time to come, tends to draw away the youth who has enjoyed it from a business life ; tends to fix his mind, tastes, thoughts upon a very different class of things from those which must make up a large part of his future as a business man and citizen. This is, of course, within certain limits an excellent thing. The man should be more than his calling. We

* Pamphlet of American Bankers' Association on Schools of Finance and Economy, November 15, 1889, p. 3.

should be men before we are anything else. We should be human beings before we are bankers, or manufacturers or lawyers or physicians, and our educational system should aim to develop all our power and tastes and possibilities—should increase our capacities for enjoyment in every direction.

But all this has reached its limit when the educational process itself has so warped individual development as to turn aside the individual from a calling for which he has special aptitude to one for which he is not at all fitted. Now no one, I think, who has been through college himself and has afterwards taught for years in a college can help admitting that the traditional college curriculum has turned aside many a boy from a business career in which he might have succeeded to a professional one in which he failed. Our college courses as they are at present constituted—considering the preparatory course as a part of the college—holds the boy who completes it during two very critical periods : the one from 12 to 16 and the other from 17 to 21 ; where he passes from childhood to youth and from youth to manhood. That a course of study pursued during these years—no matter how good it may be in itself—may warp for harm many a boy who comes under its influence, can be denied, it seems to me, only by him who thinks it possible to devise an absolutely good curriculum which will be suitable to all boys—no matter what their tastes or abilities. There are some people who hold to this view. They are fortunately, for the world, becoming fewer and fewer and losing their influence steadily.

I say these things with a full recognition of the fact that many of our most successful business men in all lines of life, banking, manufacturing, merchandising, etc., are college bred men, and that they regard themselves and probably with justice as all the better business men for the college education which they have had ; but this fact is, of course, no answer to the above propositions since the claim is not that a college education, even of the strictest old-fashioned type destroys or even weakens a man's business ability, but simply that it tends in many instances to draw men away from a business life who are naturally adapted to it; and what is of far more importance in this connection, the knowledge that such a course is all the college has to offer him deters the youth looking forward to business from going to college at all—yea—even from considering seriously the possible advantage of a collegiate training.

However, whatever one may think of the above views, and I am well aware that many people, both educationists and others, will take exception to them, I do not think that the fact can be denied that our colleges are not educating our business men as a matter of fact. The case is not so bad by any means as it was represented some time ago by Mr. Carnegie, who declared that he did not know any successful business men who are college graduates. Our larger cities, particularly, show many very successful business men who are graduates of colleges, and while I would not say that the woods are full of them, yet certainly many of our Western frontier towns can show, especially among the very young men, numerous examples of collegians successful in business. And yet, after all, there is an immense amount of truth in what Mr. Carnegie says. It may be perfectly true, as has been contended on the other hand, that the proportion of college men, who, having gone into business, are successful is immensely greater than the proportion of successful men among the non-college class; and yet be also the case, as it undoubtedly is, that of the successful business men in this country but very few are college graduates, *i. e.*, our colleges are not educating our business men. It was shown years ago that the population of this country was growing faster than the number of students in our colleges, and certainly the business classes have increased in number much more rapidly than the number of students, *i. e.*, the ratio of college men in business to the non-college men is declining. Even the proportion of college graduates in the professional schools of the country has not been increasing of late, *i. e.*, even the number of physicians and lawyers, and possibly, clergymen, who are college graduates is not relatively increasing, and indeed may be decreasing, and yet the college is considered specially adapted to these classes.

In other words, the old-fashioned college curriculum may be just the thing for the business man—may be an ideal training also for him; but if so, he does not see it and has not been persuaded of it, and from all present indications never will be. If then, it is desirable for our business men to have a higher training some other curriculum than the old-fashioned one must be devised—some course arranged which will appeal to them.

It was these considerations, then, that determined Mr. Wharton to establish this school. First: the belief that the business classes of our country need a higher training as much or more than any other classes; second, the view that the Commercial or Business College, however valuable its curriculum, is by its very nature unable to give this higher training; third, the fact that the American college, however real and valuable its higher training, does not in its present form furnish a kind of higher training which appeals to the business sentiment of the community, as is shown by the fact of the small number of youths looking to business careers who enter college.

The result of these convictions was the establishment of the Wharton School of Finance and Economy, an institution to furnish a higher training to the business classes of the community which should be at once liberal and practical.

The desirability of such facilities for higher business education may be regarded from two points of view—that of the community and that of the persons most immediately benefited by it. There can be little doubt that a liberal education of the business classes lies in the interest of the community. One of the most striking facts of modern civilization is the rapidly growing importance of the business, as distinct from the professional classes. This is plain enough even in Europe where it is still kept back by the predominance of the court, the army and the church and where the bar and physic still maintain their high position. It is, however, beyond all doubt true in this country where the great merchant prince, the railroad president, the great manufacturer and banker have succeeded to the place of power once held by the great orator, statesman, lawyer or clergyman. The professional class is losing ground, the business world gaining it. Whether for weal or woe, the control of government, of society, of education, of the press, yes, even of the church is slipping more and more rapidly into the hands of the business classes, and it is this class which to an ever increasing extent will dominate our political and social life.

The question, therefore, what their education shall be is a fundamental one to our prosperity and welfare. If it is an education which will broaden and liberalize them, enlarge their views, widen their outlook, quicken their sympathies, beget and increase a public spirit which shall find its greatest happiness in seeking out and utilizing means of promoting the common welfare, we may be sure that the interests of our society and civilization will be in good hands. If it should be the reverse of all this, then woe to us and our posterity!

Now I am not one of those who would unduly exaggerate the tendency of a higher education to produce those and similar results. I have met many men who had had the best opportunities for a liberal education afforded by Europe and America and who have come out of it with all the narrowness and selfishness of the meanest hayseed of them all; and we all know many men, of no school education worth speaking of, who were yet the very salt of the earth in all matters which call for a liberal view, for a self-sacrificing public spirit. To take a simple illustration—how much of the educational endowment of this country is owing to men who never had a chance to go to school in their lives.

And yet after making all due allowance for the narrowness of many so-called liberally educated men, and for the liberality of many so-called uneducated men, it still remains true that the higher aspects of human society —the liberal support of science and art, the intelligent direction of charity and benevolence is to be expected chiefly from an educated class, and just in proportion as our ruling sets became educated may we expect to see these finer things increase and multiply.

There is another aspect to the problem. The so-called uneducated men who through their ability, energy, and perseverance have accumulated fortunes, have found in the very necessity of sticking to business early and late a conservative force which from boyhood on, speaking in a business sense, has kept their feet in the way that they should tread. Having accumulated this fortune themselves they do not care to put their sons through the same weary round. Where shall they find for them the saving force which shall do for them in the growing years what hard work did for their fathers? It is to be found chiefly in the right sort of higher education —an education that shall fit them to take up in the right spirit the work that will fall upon their shoulders, *i. e.*, the management of property already accumulated or business already established.

I cannot agree, moreover, with those who believe that it is a good thing for fortune once accumulated to be squandered. Three generations from shirt sleeves to shirt sleeves may be an accurate description of what occurs as a matter of fact. That it should so frequently occur is, however, to be deplored. It is possible that circumstances may favor the accumulation of fortunes so great as to be a menace to the welfare of society; but aside from this circumstance, the existence of wealth for several generations in a family, if it be kept, not by artificial conditions but by the existence of qualities necessary to accumulate it in honest ways under ordinary conditions, may be a great means of bringing out the finer sides of life, of improving the strain of the stock, of raising the general level of better qualities in society. I say this with full acknowledgment of the fact that wealth produces in many cases the very opposite of all this ; but if so, it is the fault of those who have it to administer and are too shortsighted and narrow to count, as Socrates used to say, the things important which are important.

The higher education, then, of the business class lies in the interest of society as a whole. Does it lie in the interest of the future business man himself ? Looking at the problem in a broad way, as to whether a higher education can make life the better worth living, I should say perhaps there would be but little difference of opinion. The answer must be in the affirmative. If there is something soul-satisfying in striking off the narrow limitations which hedge about the life of the corner groceryman in the backwoods village, and exchanging such a career for that of the wholesale dealer in the large city with all that the latter position implies in larger opportunities for social intercourse and enjoyment, for self-improvement, and for public service ; what shall we say of the process which lifts us out of the narrow material ruts of every-day routine and enables us to share in the thoughts and feelings of the mightiest of earth's sages in all departments of human science—which fills our hearts with enthusiasm for all that is good and great in human history, fits us to enjoy the highest pleasures of the human heart and intellect ?

But can this higher education serve any practical purpose? it may be asked. We believe it can, and in a small portion of the field we are trying at Philadelphia to show how it can be done. To do it adequately over a large field would require ten or fifteen times the endowment which we have. But we have reason to be satisfied, and indeed to feel somewhat proud of the results we have thus far achieved. We feel that we have laid a foundation upon which we can build indefinitely, and are now in a position to use wisely almost any addition which may come to our income.

Our plan, as outlined in the prospectus by Mr. Wharton above referred to, embraces in brief two elements : a liberal and a practical element—the latter also being made up of two parts, a general and a special. The founder of the school had in mind two lines of work which should be pursued simultaneously and together constitute a harmonious curriculum. He wished —to use his own words—to establish an institution in which should be taught the principles underlying successful civil government, and a training should be given in the management of property. Both these ends were to be conceived in a broad spirit. In accordance with these suggestions, and following the lines indicated in the prospectus above referred to, we have organized and developed a school which, in our opinion, is calculated to serve these ends.

, The curriculum as it now stands is appended to this paper and it may not be out of place to describe here the mode of conducting the courses and the ground we aim to cover. One of the prominent elements in our curriculum is a course in American history by the distinguished historian John B. McMaster. This course runs through two years—three hours per week the first year and four hours per week the second. This is no ordinary text-book course dealing chiefly with Indian massacres, battles and Congressional speeches : while it aims, of course, to give the leading facts of our political development, of the settlement and growth of the colonies ;

of the War of the Revolution; of the war with England, with Mexico and the war between the States; yet its chief endeavor is to discover and lay bare the very heart-springs of our national existence. It is not merely the what but the why. The professor is not content with teaching what battles were fought in the French and Indian War, for example, and by whom and where: but he tries to show how it was that a French and Indian war arose at all, and why it had to be conducted as it was and how no other outcome was possible. This involves a careful study of the economic and social conditions of the time; it makes the student acquainted with the people as they were at that period; it leads him to see the enormous difference between our country to-day and our country then. He studies the means of communication which existed then; the primitive post-office, the system of highways, or rather, lack of highways; the means of getting about; the system of money, coin and paper; the kind of banks, and the way they were managed, the system of agriculture, the manufacturing system; the products, raw and manufactured, the social habits, the education of the people, etc., etc., in a word, all that is necessary to reconstruct that period in the imagination of the student and make it a part of his mental furnishing for all time to come. A basis is thus provided for comparison and by this comparative method on the other hand the acquisition and retention of the facts thus presented is made easy.

In this way each subsequent period is taken up and worked over and when the student has completed his course, he is not only familiar with the names of the Presidents, of the Governors, of the orators and statesmen of the Republic; he not only knows when the battle of the Brandywine was fought and when the treaty of peace was signed at the close of the Revolution; but he has a tolerably clear notion of the course of our country's history in each of the great departments of our national life.

He knows, for example, the history of highway improvement; how long it took the American people to appreciate the importance of good highways; the growth of knowledge and interest in road-making; the turnpike era, the rage for canal building, the effects of our great canals on the lines of material development, the importance of the Erie Canal, economically, socially, politically; the introduction of the railway and its effect on the canal and turnpike system; why the railways followed the parallels rather than the meridians; the effect of the railway system on national industry and federal centralization; the reawakened interest in the improvement of land and water ways, etc., etc.

He knows something of the educational history of the country. He knows when the great colleges took their rise; what the secondary and primary schools were a century ago; how bitter was the fight for a respectable system of school education in nearly every Northern State, to say nothing of the States south of Mason and Dixon's line; how slowly the conviction grew that popular education is necessary to the perpetuity of republican institutions; and how difficult was the struggle—by no means finished—to establish as the necessary standard of popular education something more than the three R's; how the whole idea of free public education so slowly germinating, so slowly growing, bore its first great and influential fruit in the magnificent systems of education developed in the Mississippi Valley—more especially in Michigan; how magnificently private liberality has come to the aid of the State, creating and supporting such institutions as Harvard, Yale, Columbia, Cornell, Princeton, Pennsylvania, Johns Hopkins and many others; how the Federal Government has aided in this great work—not only by its munificent land grant to which public education in all the States owes so much, but by the establishment of those wonderful scientific departments at Washington which are the admiration and envy of every foreign country.

To take another illustration, the student has a good view of our financial history. The revenue system of the Federal Government, of the States and of the communities receives much attention. The student begins with the revenue system of the Confederation, to which, of course, only brief attention is given. From 1789 on, details are carefully studied. The various tariffs are compared with reference to the rates of duty, articles taxed, fruitfulness of duties, system of administration, method of valuation, kinds of duties, *ad valorem*, specific, combined, etc., etc., in a word, all that is necessary to enable the student to get a clear idea of our tariff history, the discussions and disputes which have occurred in its course. The same thing is done for the internal revenue system, the system of direct taxes, etc.

Similar and, indeed, more detailed attention is given to the history of money and banking. A brief study is made of the money and banking system of pre-revolutionary times—a period full of interesting and instructive experiments. A careful study is made of the period from the close of the Revolution to the adoption of the present constitution; and from the discussions about the first United States bank down to the present, a detailed study of money and banking is made. This is not confined to the consideration of the two United States Banks, our present system of National Banks, and the sub-treasury system; but it extends to the system of State banks as well. It comprises not only the banks of issue but all sorts of banks—every kind of institution, indeed, that enters into the money and credit system of the country. All this on the historical side of the course; the discussion of the principles of banking belongs to a special course which will be mentioned later.

And so I might go on and take up other subjects. but this is sufficient to give you an idea of what is included within the course in American history. It means, you see, a history of the people, their origin, habits, feelings and institutions—economic, social and religious.

Side by side with this course, runs a course in the government of the United States, which being somewhat historical in character supplements the first very fully, though its object is not so much historical as expository. It embraces a careful study of the Federal Government, supplemented by a study of State and Local government. It begins with a consideration of the Federal Constitution,—article by article. Much attention is given to the discussion of disputed questions with a view of bringing out the principles underlying our system of federal government and training the student to see the fine points of constitutional law at the same time that he grows familiar with the principles of constitutional interpretation as laid down by our great jurists. This is followed by a discussion of the government and its various departments as they now exist. The same thing is then done for the State and Local government though in a briefer way. The student is thus furnished with a knowledge of his own political institutions and his relation to the government under which he lives and in which he should take a part.

The work just described in American history and American politics is work which is of value and should be of interest to every American citizen and which receives, therefore, a very unusual amount of attention in the Wharton School of Finance and Economy.

Supplementary to these courses and aiming to give a basis of comparison for careful and intelligent study are courses in foreign politics and history. The government of one or more leading foreign countries is taken up and presented point by point in comparison with our own. In this way the student increases his stock of knowledge and at the same time comes to understand our own political system better, He learns to distinguish the essential from the accidental. He sees the weak points of our own system and the strong points of others. He acquires an inextinguishable interest in our political problems and an earnest ambition to assist in their solution.

Parallel again with these courses in American history and politics, runs a line of work intended to train the student in the investigation of the underlying principles of economic, industrial and political phenomena. This includes the courses in political science, political economy, finance, money and banking. The attempt is made here to discover and set forth fundamental principles. The abstract questions are discussed, the doctrine of theory of the State, value, rent, population, wages, money, credit, taxation, free trade, protection, with the infinitude of sub questions related to them, such as paper money, bimetalism, poor laws, banks, single tax, eight-hour laws, strikes, etc. The student learns in this course the various theories in regard to these things, the various explanations offered for existing phenomena, and remedies proposed for social defects and diseases. It is in these courses that the student lays the foundation for an intelligent and independent opinion on all the burning questions of the day, whether they relate to his business in the narrow sense of the term or to the important and pressing questions of public policy in other directions.

Finally, parallel with these courses which, as will be seen, are all more or less general in their nature, are the business courses in the narrower sense of the term. These form a nucleus containing what is of interest to all business men alike. They consist of three parts: First, a course in the general theory of accounting; second, in business law; third, in business practice. The first embraces a careful study of the general principles underlying single and double entry bookkeeping, also the study of a dozen or more sets of books carefully selected from leading branches of business and representing the best practice of typical houses. A special point is made of developing the general principles and then illustrating typical variations or applications, so that the student can understand with ease any set of books he might have occasion to examine or use. The idea is not so much to make an expert bookkeeper in any one set of books or style of accounting as to train the student so that in a short time he could become expert in any position he might take; and above all so that he can understand with facility and unravel with ease any set of accounts. Another point to which much attention is directed is corporate and public accounting. It is hoped that in course of time a reasonable system of accounting can be introduced into the practice of our cities, counties and State governments.

The course in business law is also of a general nature. It comprises a study of those business forms and acts which are common to all business alike—such as the promissory note. The idea, of course, is not to make a lawyer, nor to make the lawyer indispensable, but to give the future business man knowledge enough about such things that he may know when he does need a lawyer, and to familiarize him with some of the more usual forms common to all branches of business.

The course in business practice is intended to be a study of the organization and methods of work characteristic of a few typical lines of business, selected not so much with reference to their relative money value as to their value as specimens or illustrations of the business methods and spirit of the community.

Without going further into detail, enough has been said to give an idea of the scope and aims of the school. Our methods are directed to producing so far as college training can do it, educated young men with a taste for business, vigorous, active workers, of sturdy character and independent opinion, having a lofty faith in all things good, and able to give a reason for the faith that is in them. Each student is trained to work and think for himself. He is put on the track of the best that has been written on all sides of all important questions that fall within the range of our investigations, and if he holds an opinion he is expected to know on what grounds, and to be able to express them. I said above—all this, so far as college training can do it. We must never forget that college graduates are at best a callow set and nothing can be more amusing (except when he is disgusting) than a youth just out of college who has " matured " opinions on all subjects, and one of the results of the best college training is a modesty of opinion, an open mindedness which leaves room for future growth.

Let us glance one moment before leaving this for another point, at what the Wharton School of Finance and Economy can do for the higher education of the future banker.

If a young man completes the course, he will have acquired a fairly thorough knowledge of the history and government of the people of the United States, with some knowledge of foreign politics and history, and a general view of the principles of accounting, of business laws and practice. He will also have a pretty thorough grasp of the fundamental principles of political economy, will have studied with some thoroughness, as college study goes, the land question, the labor question, the railroad question, the ballot reform, civil service reform, congressional reform, prohibition and many other similar economic and political topics. He will have had a pretty thorough course in the theory of money and credit ; will understand the arguments *pro* and *con* in regard to bimetalism and to paper money, and will know our own history on these points; can set forth the considerations in favor of and against the constitutionality of the original United States Bank ; can explain its organization and give a history of its workings and its end. He is also acquainted with the history and methods of the second bank and of our present National Banking system. He will be able to explain the various functions of a bank and the economic system of the country and describe the different kinds of banks, both here and abroad, and give a fair history of private banks in this country from 1789 to the present. He will be able to explain the workings of the money market, so far as it can be explained ; that is, he can give the various theories in regard to it, etc , etc.

All this, of course will not make him a banker. It may not quicken his sense for a good security one iota or enable him to devise a new kind of bank which shall make him wealthy. But it will contribute toward making him an educated man, knowing something more about his business than the ordinary hand-to-mouth practical man, having a wide view of the relations of his business to other lines of business and to society as a whole, and above all, an intelligent American citizen, with a quickened interest in everything that concerns his country and his time and an immensely greater desire and ability to use what he may learn and what he may earn in his business for the benefit of his fellow men.

It will doubtless have occurred to you that more instruction in the practical details of the banking business would be desirable in the curriculum. In this the Faculty would doubtless fully concur. We need very much a lecturer on banking who could give his whole time and attention to this one subject. If we had that to supplement present facilities, we should have an almost ideal course for a youth who, looking forward to a banking career, desired a higher education which should bear some relation to his future work.

In closing, it is only necessary to add that the Wharton School of Finance and Economy is an integral part of the college department of the University of Pennsylvania. Students who have completed the first two years of the college course, either classical or scientific, are admitted to the Wharton School and graduated with the Bachelor's degree after two years successful study. Those students who have studied Greek five years and Latin six before entering the school with the other studies usually embraced in the classical course to the close of the Sophomore year, receive the A. B. degree ; other students the Ph. B.

I believe that our experience at the University of Pennsylvania amply proves the feasibility of introducing into our college curriculum the elements of business, and that this feature will popularize without lowering the college, and thus strengthen its hold on the community. Wherever this sort of course can be introduced and properly equipped, it will benefit the college and public alike.

It will be seen from the above description that the bulk of the Wharton School curriculum, aside from the business course, consists of courses in history and the political and social sciences. These latter elements are also of fundamental importance in the liberal training of lawyers and in the professional training of journalists, statesmen and college professors in these subjects. Hence it comes that of the students in the Wharton School a large per cent. is made up of those who expect to enter the academic, legal, newspaper or political career.

The ideal of the Faculty, it may be said, is a great institution, comprising many different courses, one looking to business, another to journalism, still another to politics, another to the university—all composed alike of two elements: a common one, consisting of such studies as political economy, constitutional law, politics, history, etc.; and a professional one, embracing such special instruction as may be of aid to preparing the students for their particular careers. The business course itself should be subdivided according to the intention of the student, and should comprise not merely the fundamental branches we now have, but many others, such as railroading, commerce, insurance, etc.

An institution like this, with a curriculum based upon a thorough knowledge of our own vernacular, its use, literature, history, etc., with such other languages, ancient or modern, as the student might choose to take, and all based on a thorough elementary training in languages, mathematics and natural science, would be an addition to our educational system comparable in importance and influence only to the great system of technical schools which in a different field are revolutionizing our American education. It would give us also the best system of training for business, journalism, teaching—in a word for citizenship, which the world has yet seen. It would make the man or men, the family or the community who established it immortal in the educational history—not merely of this country but of the world. Who shall be the first to utilize this magnificent chance? We have begun to cultivate one corner of the field in Philadelphia, and shall press forward as rapidly as possible to its full occupation, but shall also rejoice in the meantime if some other place outstrips us in this generous race for the highest position in this great work.

I would emphasize the fact that the Wharton School of Finance and Economy as it was conceived in a broad way, so we are trying to manage it in a broad and liberal spirit—both educationally and otherwise. Our students are by no means confined to the curriculum or course outlined above. All the studies represented in the modern American University of large type and equipment are open to them if they choose to take them. To present the subjects thus open to them would be to repeat the catalogue of the University of Pennsylvania; but a brief list of some of the more important will be of interest in this connection. Leaving out of view the Medical, Dental, Veterinary and Law Schools, with over 100 professors and instructors, the college department alone, with the Faculty of Philosophy, has over 70 instructors and professors, conducting more than 225 half yearly courses in some sixty different subjects, among which may be mentioned: Hebrew (2)*; Sanskrit (2); Greek (7); Latin (8)); English (15); Anglo-Saxon (2); Gothic (2); German (6); French (6); Italian (2); Spanish (1); Philosophy (6); Psychology (6); History (13); Drawing (3); Mathematics (25); Physics (5); Chemistry (16); Zoology (11); Botany (19); Physiology (1); Geology (5); Mineralogy (3); Metallurgy (4); Mining (3); Civil Engineering (28); Mechanical Engineering (21); Architecture (6); Music (3); etc.

Surely here is range of selection large enough to suit most college boys. The possibility of selection is conditioned, of course, by the exigencies of the programme; but any of these subjects may be taken by regular stu-

*The number in parenthesis indicates the number of courses in the subject.

22

dents if the hours do not conflict and the student is physically and mentally able to take such extra work ; while special students can, of course, adapt themselves to such hours as they wish.

Permit me, then, members of the American Bankers' Association, to bespeak your interest in the Wharton School of Finance and Economy ; but still more in the great work to which it is devoted—viz., the development of a higher course of study, at once liberal and practical, which will appeal to the business sentiment of the community and the adoption of such courses in more and more of our colleges and universities.

NOTE.—For a fuller discussion of some topics connected with this general subject see :

1. A SCHOOL OF POLITICAL AND SOCIAL SCIENCE. By E. J. James, *Ethical Record*, 1890.

2. SCHOOLS OF POLITICAL AND SOCIAL SCIENCE. By E. J. James. Publications of Philadelphia Social Science Association. Philadelphia, 1886.

3. THE STUDY OF POLITICS AND BUSINESS AT THE UNIVERSITY OF PENNSYLVANIA. Philadelphia, 1889.

4. IS A COLLEGE EDUCATION ADVANTAGEOUS TO A BUSINESS MAN? By Jas. Wharton, Philadelphia, 1890.

## APPENDIX.

### THE WHARTON SCHOOL OF FINANCE AND ECONOMY.

#### UNIVERSITY OF PENNSYLVANIA.

This school was founded by Mr. Joseph Wharton, of Philadelphia, in order to provide for young men special means of training, and of correct instruction in the knowledge and in the arts of modern Finance and Economy. It serves for the University of Pennsylvania the same purposes as are served in other institutions by their Departments or Faculties of History and Politics, or by the so-called Schools of Political Science. In addition, however, to the courses usually provided in such departments, this Institution offers also a course, at once liberal and practical, which is specially designed for those who intend to enter upon business pursuits.

The founder of the School expressed the desire that it should offer facilities for obtaining,—

(1) *An adequate education in the principles underlying successful civil government.*

(2) *A training suitable for those who intend to engage in business or to undertake the management of property.*

In order to realize these objects, courses have been provided in Political Economy, Social Science, Finance, Statistics, Political Science, Administrative and Constitutional Law of the United States and of leading foreign countries, Comparative Politics, Political and Constitutional History of the

United States, Theory and Practice of Accounting, and Mercantile Law and Practice.

It will be observed that nearly all the courses above enumerated are such as may fairly lay claim to be called liberal branches, and such as every American citizen should pursue in outline at least as a preparation for the duties of citizenship.

They are, however, also studies which form a leading constituent in the special preparation for certain callings, such as the teaching of History and Politics, Journalism, Business, Public Service and Law.

The attention, therefore, of students who are looking forward to entering upon these or similar lines of work is especially invited to the facilities of this Institution.

---

## CURRICULUM.

### JUNIOR CLASS.

#### FIRST TERM.

PUBLIC LAW AND POLITICS 1.—Constitution of the United States. *Three hours* (*First Term*). *Mon., Th., at* 11, *Tu. at* 12. Professor JAMES.

BUSINESS LAW AND PRACTICE 1.—Methods of Accounting. *Two hours. Mon. at* 12, *Tu. at* 9, *Wed. at* 1, *Fri. at* 9. Dr. FALKNER.

HISTORY 7.—American Political and Social History. Colonial History. History of the Public Domain. Distribution of Population (*Outline* printed for the class). Preparation of Boundary, Population, and Economic Maps. *Three hours* (*First Term*). *Tu. at* 11, *Wed., Th., at* 10. *Wharton School Congress meets once each week.* Professor MCMASTER.

HISTORY 8.—Church and State in America (Lectures). *Two hours* (*First Term*). *Mon. at* 10, *Wed. at* 11. Professor THOMPSON.

ECONOMICS AND SOCIAL SCIENCE 1.—Political Economy. Walker's *Political Economy* and Adam Smith's *Wealth of Nations. Three hours* (*First Term*). *Mon., Wed., at* 9, *Tu. at* 10. Professor PATTEN.

ECONOMICS AND SOCIAL SCIENCE 3.—Social Science. Thompson's *Elements of Political Economy. Two hours. Th. at* 9, *Fri. at* 11. Professor THOMPSON.

PHILOSOPHY 1.—Logic. Lectures and Recitations. Jevons' *Lessons in Logic. Two hours* (*First Term*). *Wed. at* 12, *Fri. at* 10. Professor FULLERTON.

#### SECOND TERM.

PUBLIC LAW AND POLITICS 3.—History and Theory of the State. *One hour.* (*Second Term*). *Tu. at* 12. Professor JAMES.

PUBLIC LAW AND POLITICS 4.—Constitutions of leading foreign countries. *Two hours* (*Second Term*). *Mon., Th., at* 11. Professor JAMES.

PUBLIC LAW AND POLITICS 2.—State Constitutional Law. *Two hours* (*Second Term*). Dr. THORPE.

BUSINESS LAW AND PRACTICE 1.—Methods of Accounting. *Two hours. Mon. at* 12, *Tu. at* 9, *Wed. at* 1, *Fri. at* 9. Dr. FALKNER.

HISTORY 9.—American Political and Social History (Washington to Jackson). Lectures, Maps, *Outline* printed for the class. *Three hours* (*Second Term*). *Tu. at* 11, *Wed., Th., at* 10. *Wharton School Congress meets once each week.* Professor MCMASTER.

HISTORY 10.—Economic History of the United States. *Two hours (Second Term).* *Mon. at 10, Wed. at 11.* Professor THOMPSON.

ECONOMICS AND SOCIAL SCIENCE 2.—Currency and Banking. Jevons' Money and the Mechanism of Exchange. *Three hours (Second Term).* *Mon., Wed., at 9, Tu. at 10.* Professor PATTEN.

PHILOSOPHY 2.—Ethics. Lectures and Recitations. *Two hours (Second Term), Wed. at 12, Fri. at 10.* Professor FULLERTON.

## SENIOR CLASS.

### FIRST TERM.

PUBLIC LAW AND POLITICS 5.—Public Administration in the United States. *Two hours (First Term).* *Mon. at 12, Th. at 10.* Professor JAMES.

ECONOMICS AND SOCIAL SCIENCE 7.—Revenue System in the United States and leading foreign countries. *Two hours (First Term).* *Wed., Fri., at 11.* Professor JAMES.

BUSINESS LAW AND PRACTICE 2.—Mercantile Law. Parsons' *Law of Business.* *Two hours (First Term).* *Mon. at 11, Tu, at 12.* Dr. FALKNER.

ECONOMICS AND SOCIAL SCIENCE 4.—Social Science. Lectures and Compositions. *Three hours (First Term).* *Mon. at 11, Fri. at 10.* Professor THOMPSON.

ECONOMICS AND SOCIAL SCIENCE 5.—Political Economy. Mill's *Political Economy.* *Three hours (First Term).* *Tu., Th. at 9, Wed. at 10.* Professor PATTEN.

HISTORY 13.—American Political and Social History (1825–1889). Lectures, Maps. *Four hours (First Term).* *Mon., Tu., at 10, Wed. at 12, Th. at 11. Wharton School Congress meets once each week.* Professor MCMASTER.

### SECOND TERM.

PUBLIC LAW AND POLITICS 6.—Public Administration in leading foreign countries. *Two hours (Second Term).* *Mon. at 12, Th. at 10.* Professor JAMES.

BUSINESS LAW AND PRACTICE 3.—Mercantile Practice. Lectures. *Two hours (Second Term).* *Mon. at 11, Tu. at 12.* Mr. FALKNER.

ECONOMICS AND SOCIAL SCIENCE 6.—Political Economy. Ingram's *History of Political Economy.* *Three hours (Second Term).* *Tu., Th. at 9. Wed. at 10.* Professor PATTEN.

ECONOMICS AND SOCIAL SCIENCE 8.—History and Theories of Public Finance, especially of Taxation. *Two hours (Second Term).* *Wed., Fri. at 11.* Professor JAMES.

ECONOMICS AND SOCIAL SCIENCE 9.—Statistics. General Theory. Statistics of Population. Lectures. *Two hours (Second Term).* Dr. FALKNER.

HISTORY 14.—American Constitutional History (1776–1889). Diplomatic History. Biography of American Statesmen. Lectures. *Three hours (Second Term).* *Tu. at 10, Wed. at 12, Th. at 11.* Professor MCMASTER.

HISTORY 15.—Seminary of American History. Constitutional History of the United States. *Two hours.* Professor MCMASTER.

## METHODS OF WORK.

The plan for instruction embraces recitations, lectures and seminaries. The endeavor is made to train the students to think independently on the topics that form the subjects of instruction. An earnest effort is made to exclude all dogmatism in political or economic teaching, to present fairly all aspects of disputed questions, and to put the students in a position to form their own opinions on intelligent grounds.

The advanced students receive special attention and assistance in the seminaries, which are organized to promote correct habits of work and to foster a spirit of original investigation.

In order to quicken interest in political and economical subjects, and to encourage acquaintance with parliamentary procedure, a congress has been formed in the school. It is divided into Senate and House, and adopts the rules of procedure of the respective houses, following the course of Congressional debate and action, but confining itself to a few leading topics.

## FELLOWSHIPS.

Five honorary Fellowships, which confer the privilege of attending any of the economic and historical courses of the University free of charge, are assigned at the beginning of each year. Graduates of any American college, or of foreign schools of similar grade, are eligible for appointment.

## AUXILIARY FACILITIES.

All the courses in the other departments of the College, embracing those usually found in the graduate and undergraduate courses of our best Universities, are open to students of the Wharton School without extra charge for tuition, so far as this is consistent with their roster of studies in the School.

The following courses given in the Law School are of special interest to students in this department:—

1. Roman Law.
2. Constitutional Law of the United States.
3. International Law.
4. History of the Common Law.

Besides the University Library, which has an unusually valuable collection of works on economics and statistics, the public libraries of the city, and many of the private ones also, aggregating several hundred thousand volumes, are open to the students in the pursuit of their University work.

## PUBLICATIONS.

A series of occasional publications on Political Economy and Public Law and on History will be issued by the University, representing a portion of the work done in the seminaries by the professors and students. The following numbers have already appeared :—1. Wharton School Annals of Political Science. 2. The Anti-Rent Agitation in New York. 3. Ground Rents in Philadelphia. 4. Consumption of Wealth. 5. Prison Statistics in 1888. 6. Rational Principles of Taxation. 7. German Constitution. 8. Swiss Constitution.

## LIBRARY.

The University possesses a large and valuable library of works relating to finance and political economy. The foundation was laid by the great collection of the late Stephen Colwell, comprising between seven and eight thousand volumes, and including nearly every important book on these subjects in the English, French, and Italian languages, published before 1860. This collection has been supplemented by the bequest of the library of the late Henry C. Carey, which includes many later works and pamphlets, and is especially rich in statistical literature, European government reports, and the like. It embraces a collection of about three thousand English pamphlets, formerly Mr. McCalmont's, covering the period from the close of the seventeenth century to our own times, and bound in chronological order. Mr. Joseph Wharton has recently increased his benefactions to the School by a gift of twenty-five thousand dollars to establish a fund for the purchase of books in economics and politics.

)Original research by the students, under the direction of the professors, is a part of the work of the School.

RESOLUTION OF EXECUTIVE COUNCIL OF THE AMERICAN BANKERS'
ASSOCIATION, AT THEIR MEETING ON OCTOBER 16, 1889 IN
NEW YORK CITY.

INTRODUCING PLAN OF THE

# WHARTON SCHOOL OF FINANCE AND ECONOMY

## OF THE UNIVERSITY OF PENNSYLVANIA.

On motion of WILLIAM H. RHAWN, it was

*Resolved*, That a Committee of not less than three, or more than five, be appointed by the chairman, to whom shall be submitted the subject of the preparation or procurement of a paper to be read at the next Convention of the Association upon the establishment of schools in connection with the universities and colleges of the country, of general scope and character like that of " The Wharton School of Finance and Economy " connected with the University of Pennsylvania ; and the best means by which the establishment and endowment of such schools may be promoted and fostered by the Association.

The Chairman, the Hon. JOHN JAY KNOX, appointed on above Committee, Mr. WILLIAM H. RHAWN, Mr. LOGAN C. MURRAY and Mr. MORTON MCMICHAEL.

To explain the intention and scope of Mr. Rhawn's resolution, the following statement is made :

In May, 1881, Mr. Joseph Wharton, the founder of the Wharton School of Finance and Economy, sent to the Trustees of the University of Pennsylvania the address and project hereto attached, marked Plan of the Wharton School.

Those Trustees having decided to accept the proffered endowment, and to establish the School, Mr. Wharton transferred to them on June 22, 1881, the fund of $100,000,* and a contract was executed between him and the said Trustees, to which was attached a copy of the above-mentioned address and project in order to exhibit in full the conditions of the endowment. That contract bound the University to carry out the enterprise on the lines thus laid down, and it provided that by Mr. Wharton during his lifetime, and by the Judges of the Philadelphia Courts of Common Pleas after his death, a visitor might be appointed who should have authority to inspect the workings of the School.

With the commencement of the next term at the University this School was opened, and was at first but moderately successful. The proposed course of instruction was novel and did not apparently open an immediate career to the graduates ; the requirements for admission and for study being at first thought easier than in other departments of the University those other departments had superior attractions for the most vigorous young men ; the professors and instructors must needs feel their way at first, and gradually form both themselves and the School.

But, by steady perseverance in its task, the School has constantly improved in the thoroughness of its instruction, and has so demonstrated its

---

* Mr. Wharton has since added $25,000 for a library.

usefulness that it is now chosen by many of the most earnest students, and ranks as high as any other department in the mental discipline it imparts.

Its peculiar and special line of work naturally draws to it students with many aims and from many quarters. Japan, for instance, has from the first had one or more representatives in the School; the present United States Minister to Brazil studied here.

Although the extensive libraries of the late Hon. Henry C. Carey and the late Hon. Stephen Colwell, as well as sundry other valuable contributions of books, were placed at the disposition of this School, the necessity for continued accession of new publications became apparent, and on October 4, 1889, Mr. Wharton made a further endowment of $25,000—in six per cent. bonds—to found a library fund. The income derived from the said bonds or from any reinvestment of the fund to be applied to the purchase of such books, periodicals, documents or publications as have a special bearing on the subjects which by the deed of gift founding the School are to be therein taught.

As the corps of professors and instructors has been improved by gradual selection and training into a really capable and efficient Faculty, so has the tone of the students been elevated. At present admission is of those who, after passing two years in the general Freshman and Sophomore classes of the University, have elected to spend their Junior and Senior two years in this School.

It seems reasonable to expect not only for this School a career of real service to the community, but for other schools to be established elsewhere on similar lines, a large part in the future education of this country.

### Plan of the Wharton School.

To the Trustees of the University of Pennsylvania:

The general conviction that college education did little toward fitting for the actual duties of life any but those who purposed to become lawyers, doctors, or clergymen, brought about the creation of many excellent technical and scientific schools, whose work is enriching the country with a host of cultivated minds prepared to overcome all sorts of difficulties in the world of matter.

Those schools, while not replacing the outgrown and obsolescent system of apprenticeship, accomplish a work quite beyond anything that system was capable of. Instead of teaching and perpetuating the narrow, various, and empirical routines of certain shops, they base their instruction upon the broad principles deduced from all human knowledge, and ground in science, as well as in art, pupils who are thereby fitted both to practice what they have learned and to become themselves teachers and discoverers.

In the matter of commercial education there was formerly a system of instruction practiced in the counting-houses of the old-time merchants resembling the system of apprenticeship to trades. Comparatively few examples of this sort of instruction remain, nor is their deficiency made good by the so-called Commercial Colleges, for however valuable may be the knowledge which they impart, it does not suffice to fit a young man for the struggle of commercial life, for wise management of a private estate, or for efficient public service.

It is obvious that training in a commercial house not of the first rank for magnitude and intelligence must, like trade apprenticeship, often result in narrowness and empiricism which are not compensated by the hard and practical certainty within limited bounds derived from the routine of trade or business. Since systematic instruction cannot be expected from the overworked heads of any great establishment, the novice mostly depends on what he can gather from the salaried employés of the house, and, instead of being instructed in the various branches, is probably kept working at some particular function for which he has shown aptitude, or where his service is most needed. Besides, ordinary prudence requires that many things indispensable to mastery of the business should be kept secret from these novices.

There is, furthermore, in this country, an increasing number of young men possessing, by inheritance, wealth, keenness of intellect and latent power of command or organization, to whom the channels of commercial education, such as it is, are, by the very felicity of their circumstances, partly closed, for when they leave college at the age of twenty to twenty-five years they are already too old to be desirable beginners in a counting-house, or to descend readily to its drudgery.

No country can afford to have this inherited wealth and capacity wasted for want of that fundamental knowledge which would enable the possessors to employ them with advantage to themselves and to the community, yet how numerous are the instances of speedy ruin to great estates, and indolent waste of great powers for good simply for want of such knowledge and of the tastes and self-reliance which it brings. Nor can any country long afford to have its laws made and its government administered by men who lack such training as would suffice to rid their minds of fallacies, and qualify them for the solution of the social problems incident to our civilization. Evidently a great boon would be bestowed upon the nation if its young men of inherited intellect, means and refinement could be more generally led so to manage their property as, while husbanding it, to benefit the community, or could be drawn into careers of unselfish legislation and administration.

As the possession of any power is usually accompanied by taste for its exercise, it is reasonable to expect that adequate education in the principles underlying successful business management and civil government would greatly aid in producing a class of men likely to become most useful members of society, whether in private or in public life. An opportunity for good seems here to exist similar to that so largely and profitably availed of by the technical and scientific schools.

These considerations, joined to the belief that one of the existing great universities, rather than an institution of lower rank, or a new independent establishment, should lead in the attempt to supply this important deficiency in our present system of education, have led me to suggest the project herewith submitted, for the establishment of a School of Finance and Economy as a Department of the University which you now control, and which seems well suited to undertake a task so accordant with its general aims. In order that the University may not, by undertaking it, assume a pecuniary burden, I hereby propose to endow the School with the securities below named, amounting to $100,000, and yielding more than $6000 annual interest; these securities not to be converted during my lifetime without my assent, and no part of the endowment to be at any time invested in any obligation of the University, viz.:

$50,000 stock in the Delaware and Bound Brook Railroad Company.

$50,000 mortgage bonds of the Schuylkill Navigation Company, due in 1907.

I am prepared to convey these securities at the opening of the first term of the School, or at any earlier time when the University shall satisfy me that the School will surely be organized as below stated, and opened at the beginning of the next term, interest being adjusted to such time of opening.

The only conditions which I impose are that the University shall establish and maintain the School according to the tenor of the "Project" hereto appended, and that if the University shall at any time hereafter, by its own desire, or by default establish in a suitable Court of Equity, cease so to maintain the School, or if the School shall fail to attract students and therefore prove in the judgment of such Court to be of inconsiderable utility, the endowment shall forthwith revert to me or to my heirs, I reserving the right during my life to amend in any way, with the assent of the then Trustees of the University, the terms of the said " Project."

To commemorate a family name which has been honorably borne in this community since the foundation of the city, I desire that the School shall be called " The Wharton School of Finance and Economy."

THE PROJECT.

1. *Object.* To provide for young men special means of training and of correct instruction in the knowledge and in the arts of modern Finance and Economy, both public and private, in order that, being well informed and free from delusions upon these important subjects, they may either serve the community skillfully as well as faithfully in offices of trust, or, remaining in private life, may prudently manage their own affairs and aid in maintaining sound financial morality: in short, to establish means for imparting a liberal education in all matters concerning Finance and Economy.

2. *Qualifications for Admission.* Assuming that the special instruction of this School will occupy three years, which may be called the sub-junior, junior, and senior years, the general qualifications for admission to the sub-junior class should be equal to those for the corresponding class in the Towne Scientific School, but different in detail to the extent required by the difference in studies to be thenceforward pursued.

As preparatory to admission to that class, candidates may at the discretion of the Trustees of the University, be received into either of the lower classes of the Department of Arts, or of the Towne Scientific School, upon the same general conditions as shall, from time to time, be established for admission to those classes. To guard against the too frequent unsoundness of preliminary instruction, which is a vice of our time, and which affords no proper foundation for a collegiate course, honest fulfillment must be exacted of those reasonable detailed conditions for admission which shall, from time to time, be determined upon and set forth in the official catalogue.

3. *Organization.* The School to be conducted by—

(*a*) One principal or dean, to exercise general control over the whole School and to give tone to the instruction. He should, besides taking such part as may be found expedient in the routine instruction of the various classes, give stated and formal lectures, constituting a part of the instruction of the graduating class, and should in each year produce for publication a treatise upon some topic of current public interest connected with the lines of study pursued in the School, which treatises should be of such nature as to bring reputation to the School, and to possess permanent value as a series. No such treatise to be published until approved by a committee of the Board of Trustees appointed for that purpose, a certificate of their examination and approval to be printed at the beginning of the treatise.

(*b*) One professor or instructor of accounting or bookkeeping, to teach the simplest and most practical forms of bookkeeping for housekeepers, for private individuals, for commercial and banking firms, for manufacturing establishments, and for banks; also, the modes of keeping accounts by executors, trustees, and assignees, by the officials of towns and cities, as well as by the several departments of a State or National Government; also, the routine of business between a bank and a customer.

(*c*) One professor or instructor upon money and currency, to teach the meaning, history, and functions of money and currency, showing particularly the necessity of permanent uniformity or integrity in the coin unit upon which the money system of a nation is based; how an essential attribute of money is that it should be hard to get; the nature of, and reasons for, interest, or hire of money, and rents; the advantages of an adequate precious-metal fund for settling international balances as well as for regulating and checking by redemption the paper money and credits of a modern commercial nation; how such metallic hoards are amassed and defended; the extent to which paper money may be advantageously employed; the distinctions between bank-notes and Government notes; the uses and abuses of credit, both private and public; the uses and abuses of bills of exchange, letters of credit, and promissory notes; the history of banking, and particularly of Government banks; the advantages and dangers of banks of issue, banks of deposit and savings banks; how the functions of different sorts of banks may be combined in one, and how any of them may be banks of discount; the functions of clearing-houses; the phenomena and causes of panics and money crises; the nature of pawn establishments and of lotteries; the nature of stocks and bonds, with the ordinary modes of dealing therein.

(*d*) One Professor or Instructor upon Taxation, to teach the history and practice of modern taxation as distinguished from the plunder, tribute, or personal service which it for the most part replaces; the proper objects and rates of taxation for municipal, State, or National purposes; the public ends for which money may properly be raised by taxation; the nature of direct and indirect taxation, of excise, of customs or import duties, of export duties, of stamps, of income tax; the modern methods by which taxes are usually levied; the influences exercised upon the morality and prosperity of a community or nation by the various modes and extents of taxation; the effects upon taxation of wars and of standing armies; the extent to which corporations should be encouraged by the State and to what extent they should be taxed as compared with individuals engaged in similar pursuits.

(e) One Professor or Instructor upon Industry, Commerce and Transportation, to teach how industries advance in excellence, or decline, and shift from place to place; how by intelligent industry nations or communities thrive; how by superior skill and diligence some nations grow rich and powerful, and how by idleness or ill-directed industry others become rude and poor; how a great nation should be as far as possible self-sufficient, maintaining a proper balance between agriculture, mining and manufactures, and supplying its own wants; how mutual advantage results from reciprocal exchange of commodities natural to one land for the diverse commodities natural to another, but how by craft in commerce one nation may take the substance of a rival and maintain for itself virtual monopoly of the most profitable and civilizing industries; how by suitable tariff legislation a nation may thwart such designs, may keep its productive industry active, cheapen the cost of commodities, and oblige foreigners to sell to it at low prices while contributing largely toward defraying the expenses of its government; also, the nature and origin of money wages; the necessity, for modern industry, of organizing under single leaders and employers great amounts of capital and great numbers of laborers, and of maintaining discipline among the latter; the proper division of the fruits of organized labor between capitalist, leader, and workman; the nature and prevention of "strikes;" the importance of educating men to combine their energies for the accomplishment of any desirable object, and the principles upon which such combinations should be effected.

(f) One Professor or Instructor upon Elementary and Mercantile Law, to teach the Constitution of the United States and of Pennsylvania; the principal features of the United States law concerning industry, commerce, navigation and land and mining titles; the principal features of the laws of Pennsylvania and of other States concerning mercantile affairs, partnerships and corporations; of so-called international law; of the law of common carriers; the nature and operation of fire, marine and life insurance; the principal features of State law concerning inheritance, conveyance of land titles, mortgages and liens; in brief, the history and present status of commercial legislation and the directions in which improvements may be hoped and striven for, particularly as to harmonizing, or unifying under United States laws, the diverse legislation of the several States of this Nation; the manner of conducting stockholders' and directors' meetings as well as public meetings, the rules governing parliamentary assemblies, the routine and forms of legislative bodies.

Elocution should be taught and practiced to the extent of habituating the students to clear, forcible and unembarrassed utterance before an audience of whatever they may have to say, not in such manner as to promote mere rhetoric or prettiness. Athletic exercise within moderate limits should be encouraged, as tending to vigor and self-reliance. Latin, German and French, and sound general knowledge of mathematics, geography, history and other branches of an ordinary good education must be acquired by the students, but these points are not here dwelt upon, because it is desired to direct attention to the peculiar features of the School.

This sketch of the instruction to be given in the School is not to be regarded as precisely defining, much less as limiting, that which shall be there undertaken and carried on, but rather as indicating its general scope and tendency ; the true intent and meaning being that instruction shall be carefully provided for and regularly given in this School at least as full and thorough as is above set forth, and substantially as there stated.

All the teaching must be clear, sharp and didactic; not uncertain nor languid. The students must be taught and drilled, not lectured to without care whether or not attention is paid; any lazy or incompetent student must be dismissed.

Though the special Curriculum should probably at first be arranged to occupy three years, as has been suggested above, this term might hereafter be extended, or post-graduate instruction introduced, if experience should so dictate.

The Dean, and Professors or Instructors, are to constitute the Faculty of the School, and are to administer its discipline, as is done by the Dean and Faculty of the other Departments of the University, subject to such general rules as shall from time to time be established for the University by the Board of Trustees.

4. *General tendency of Instruction.* This should be such as to inculcate and impress upon the students :

(*a*) The immorality and practical inexpediency of seeking to acquire wealth by winning it from another, rather than by earning it through some sort of service to one's fellow-men.

(*b*) The necessity of system and accuracy in accounts, of thoroughness in whatever is undertaken, and of strict fidelity in trusts.

(*c*) Caution in contracting private debt directly or by endorsement, and in incurring obligation of any kind ; punctuality in payment of debt and in performance of engagements. Abhorrence of repudiation of debt, or inconsiderate incurring of public debt.

(*d*) The deep comfort and healthfulness of pecuniary independence, whether the scale of affairs be small or great. The consequent necessity of careful scrutiny of income and outgo, whether private or public, and of such management as will cause the first to exceed, even if but slightly, the second. In national affairs, this applies not only to the public treasury, but also to the mass of the nation, as shown by the balance of trade.

(*e*) The necessity of rigorously punishing by legal penalties and by social exclusion those persons who commit frauds, betray trusts, or steal public funds, directly or indirectly. The fatal consequences to a community of any weak toleration of such offenses must be most distinctly pointed out and enforced.

(*f*) The fundamental fact that the United States is a nation, composed of populations wedded together for life, with full power to enforce internal obedience, and not a loose bundle of incoherent communities living together temporarily without other bond than the humor of the moment.

(*g*) The necessity for each nation to care for its own, and to maintain by all suitable means its industrial and financial independence; no apologetic or merely defensive style of instruction must be tolerated upon this point, but the right and duty of national self-protection must be firmly asserted and demonstrated.

5. *Theses and Premiums.* Each student intending to graduate should prepare an original thesis upon some topic germane to the instruction of the school, such as The great currents of the world's exchanges, past and present; The existing revenue system of Great Britain, France, Mexico, Japan, or some other modern nation ; The revenue system, at some definite period, of Athens, Rome, Venice, or other ancient or mediæval nation ; The relative advantages of mono-metallic and of bi-metallic money ; The Latin monetary union ; The land-credit banks of Germany; Life insurance, tontines, annuities, and endowments; Reciprocity and commercial treaties ; The nature of French Sociétés generales, anonymes, and en commandite; The banking system past or present, of some specified nation ; The advantages and disadvantages of attempts by employers to provide for the wants of their workmen beyond payment of stipulated wages.

In style the theses should be lucid, terse, and sincere, showing mastery of the subject, with appropriate and logical arrangement of parts, leading up to definite statement of conclusions reached. The chirography must be neat and legible.

For the best thesis, and also for the best general proficiency in the studies taught in the School, should be given annually a gold medal weighing about one ounce, to be called respectively " Founder's Thesis Medal," and " Founder's Proficiency Medal," the same to be awarded by the Dean and Professors or Instructors in council.

6. *Relations to the University.* This school is intended to form an integral part of the University of Pennsylvania, its Dean and Professors or Instructors to be appointed by the Trustees of that University, its functions to be exercised under the general oversight of the Provost and Trustees, and its specific course of instruction to be determined by them ; its diplomas to be countersigned by him ; its funds, however, to be kept absolutely distinct from those of the University, and to be kept separately invested by the Trustees of the University in the name of this School, to be applied only to its own uses and not encroached upon in any manner for any debt, engagement, need, or purpose of the University.

Since this School will require no house accommodation except for class rooms, the use of which it is expected the University will freely grant, none of its funds must be expended in building or for rent-paying.

7. *Financial Prospectus.* An endowment capable of yielding $6000 per annum would seem to be necessary and adequate. Forty students, if at $150 per annum each would contribute a similar sum.

From this revenue of $12,000 per annum the Dean might be paid $3000, and each of the five professors or Instructors $1500 per annum, thus consuming $10,500 and leaving $1500 per annum from which to accumulate gradually a Safety Fund equal to at least one year's expenses, also to buy books and to pay for premiums and for publication of treatises. The interest of this Safety Fund might properly be applied to pay to the Treasury of the School for the tuition of those admitted to free scholarships ; the number of which would thus be limited by the amount of such interest, but, besides the other requisites for admission, sound physical health and high probability of life must be indispensable conditions for the enjoyment of a free scholarship.

Before so many as forty students are in attendance the number of instructors may be reduced by running the subjects together. When more than forty attend, the instruction may be expanded, the salaries advanced, or the Safety Fund increased, as the Trustees may think most expedient. During the first years, before all the classes are under tuition, the instruction will naturally be condensed, fewer Professors or Instructors perhaps be required, and the Safety Fund thus have opportunity for accumulation. It is not expected that the University shall consume its own means for the support of this School, further than to provide class rooms.

The School must exemplify its teachings by always keeping its expenses surely within its income, except that in emergencies it may consume any part of the principal of the Safety Fund, the same to be afterward replaced as soon as practicable.

PROCEEDINGS OF THE AMERICAN BANKERS' ASSOCIATION RELATIVE TO
ADDRESS OF PROFESSOR JAMES, AND UPON THE FOUNDING OF

## SCHOOLS OF FINANCE AND ECONOMY.

*First Day, September Third, Page 42 of " Proceedings."*

President CHARLES PARSONS in the Chair:

Mr. BUTTS—Before we proceed further I desire to state that we have listened with great pleasure to the able and interesting paper of Professor James, and I think this Convention would do itself justice in tendering to him a vote of thanks and directing that his paper be printed. I make that motion.

Mr. R. M. NELSON—I second that motion.

Mr. N. B. VAN SLYKE—I would suggest an amendment, that the Secretary be directed to publish 2000 copies of Mr. James' paper for circulation among our members.

Mr. BUTTS—I accept that amendment.

Mr. WM. H. RHAWN—I would suggest that there be no restriction placed upon the Secretary as to the number of copies to be printed. Let that be left to the judgment of the Executive Council.

Mr. VAN SLYKE—I have no objection to that, and being located where the State University is situated in Wisconsin, I have presented this same subject there.

The PRESIDENT—then the motion is, that the thanks of this Convention be tendered to Professor James for his address, and that the Executive Council be requested to publish a sufficient number of copies not in the regular report for distribution among members.

Mr. RHAWN—I think, in order to make that more complete, that the plan of the Wharton School should be published with the paper.

Mr. BUTTS—I will include that in my motion.

The PRESIDENT—Gentlemen, you all understand the motion. All in favor of it will vote Aye. Carried.

*Second Day, September Fourth, Pages 65-68 of " Proceedings."*

Mr. RHAWN—Now, if is in order, I would like to offer a resolution to be referred to the Executive Council.

The PRESIDENT—It is not in regular order, but if there is no objection you may offer it now.

Mr. RHAWN—I take much satisfaction to myself for the appearance of Professor James before the Convention yesterday, inasmuch as I was to some extent instrumental in getting him here ; and I was greatly pleased that the Convention should not only have unanimously voted him the thanks of this Association for his admirable address, but ordered it to be printed, with the plan of the Wharton School in separate, pamphlet form, as well as with the regular Proceedings of the Convention, thereby manifesting the deep interest felt in the subject by the Association, in regard to which I desire to offer a couple of resolutions for reference to the Executive Council, prefacing them with two paragraphs from the closing remarks of Professor James:

"The ideal of the Faculty, it may be said, is a great institution, comprising many different courses, one looking to business, another to journalism, still another to politics, another to the university—all composed alike of two elements: a common one, consisting of such studies as political economy, constitutional law, politics, history, etc,; and a professional one, embracing such special instructions as may be of aid in preparing the students for their particular careers. The business course itself should be subdivided according to the intention of the student, and should comprise not merely the fundamental branches we now have, but many others, such as railroading, commerce, insurance, etc."

"An institution like this, with a curriculum based upon a thorough knowledge of our own vernacular, its use, literature, history, etc., with such other languages, ancient or modern, as the student might choose to take, and all based on a thorough elementary training in languages, mathematics and natural science, would be an addition to our educational system comparable in importance and influence only to the great system of technical schools which in a different field are revolutionizing our American education. It would give us also the best system of training for business, journalism, teaching—in a word for citizenship, which the world has yet seen. It would make the man or men, the family or the community who established it immortal in the educational history—not merely in this country but of the world. Who shall be the first to utilize this magnificent chance? We have begun to cultivate one corner of the field in Philadelphia, and shall press forward as rapidly as possible to its full occupation, but shall also rejoice in the meantime if some other place outstrips us in this generous race for the highest position in this great work."

The resolutions which I wish to offer are as follows:

*Resolved,* "That the American Bankers' Association most earnestly commends not only to the bankers but to all intelligent and progressive citizens throughout our country the founding of schools of finance and economy for the business training of our children, to be established in connection with the universities and colleges of the land, upon a like general plan as that of the Wharton School of the University of Pennsylvania, so ably set forth by Professor James in his most admirable address before this Association ; and, as was so well stated by Professor James, the establishment of a great institution for the business training and education, such as he most vividly portrayed, would give us the best system of training for business, journalism—in a word, for citizenship, which the world has yet seen, and would make the man or the men, the family or community who established it immortal, not merely of this country, but of the world, and, as the founding of such an institution is a work which should peculiarly commend itself to the most serious consideration of the American banker, therefore,

*Resolved,* "That the Executive Council is hereby directed to carefully consider and devise a feasible plan whereby this Association may enter upon or promote such work, and report upon the same at the next Convention."

A MEMBER—I second the resolution of Mr. Rhawn.

The PRESIDENT—Mr. Atkinson is intimately acquainted with this subject, and, if agreeable, he will say a word or two about it.

Mr. EDWARD ATKINSON—Gentlemen, I am delighted to see a move of this sort brought before you. I desire to say a word to sustain it. I have been until the present year for more than twenty years a director in the

Massachusetts Institute of Technology. My brother, lately deceased, was the professor of English. It had been a hobby of ours for many years to establish a branch of training for the higher education of young men for commercial life. We were qualified, most of us, to direct that institution by what we did not know more than by what we did, but what we ought to have known in order to have been prepared to conduct our own business. For more than twenty years I have been in correspondence notably with Professor Hodgson, now deceased, of the University of Edinburgh, where they had a distinct branch of this sort, and with other prominent educators. We have, both in the Institute of Technology and in the Harvard College elective courses of instruction which have been framed with this motive in view. A backbone of science and of languages coupled with instruction in commercial geography and geology, and in English, with lectures on the principles of the law of contracts and all the preliminary methods of studies, but they are as yet departments. There is room and a field for separate schools like that of the Wharton School attached to universities, and I am delighted to see this movement made to extend the functions of education in the directions in which I myself and many of my friends have been working most arduously for very many years. (Applause.)

Mr. MORTON MCMICHAEL of Philadelphia—The Association owes to the good judgment, energy and care of Mr. Rhawn the fact that this matter of business schools has been brought to its attention so clearly, and much is yet to be learned on the subject. One point which has not been alluded to strikes me as of no small importance—that is the moral effect on the students. Young men carefully trained for years to look with shame and contempt upon the slightest deviation from strict integrity in any transaction would, I believe, acquire a very firm foundation of honesty, making them exceptionally trustworthy in positions of responsibility. The lad who enters West Point is no braver than his fellows, but years of constant teaching that personal honor is all important and that its highest expression is unfaltering courage and unswerving fidelity to duty, instils into his being a quality which makes him a braver man in the face of danger, and one more certain to carry out his orders without counting the cost to himself.

So, I am satisfied, men educated in such colleges as are proposed would have a greater fund of strength to resist temptations which so often lead to ruin and disgrace.

Mr. THOMPSON of Tacoma, Wash.—I desire to submit this proposition. I come from the extreme West, from a section which is to be the seat of great industrial and commercial activity. I am not a college man. I wish I were. But observation has taught me that in the colleges and universities there are vast stores of knowledge to be obtained, but not that kind of knowledge which permits of application to the business affairs of life. If I understand the object of these schools, it is to teach men to apply the knowledge they gather in the colleges to the business affairs of life. That is what we need. It is the making of practical men. I thoroughly advocate this measure. I would like to see in the State of Washington a school of this sort become a part of our State University, and it shall certainly become a part of my business to advocate this work. I do not believe this

Convention can do better than to take up subjects of this kind, and I am glad we have had Mr. Atkinson here to-day to confirm this, as well as Professor James yesterday. I hope the resolution will be carried unanimously, and that it will not be lost sight of in future conventions.

The PRESIDENT—Gentlemen, you have heard the resolution. All in favor of adoption will vote Aye.

Adopted unanimously.

*Third Day, September Fifth, Pages 105–106 " Proceedings."*

Mr. WM. H. RHAWN—I have a short report from the Executive Council, which I will read, as follows:

In reference to the resolution offered by Mr. Wm. H. Rhawn, the Executive Council unanimously recommend the adoption of the following by the Convention:

*Resolved*, That the American Bankers' Association most earnestly commends, not only to the bankers, but to all intelligent and progressive citizens throughout the country, the founding of Schools of Finance and Economy, for the business training of youth, to be established in connection with the universities and colleges of the land, upon a general plan like that of the Wharton School of Finance and Economy of the University of Pennsylvania, so ably set forth by Professor James in his most admirable address before this Convention.

*Resolved*, That the Executive Council is hereby directed to carefully consider, and, if possible, devise some feasible plan whereby this Association may encourage or promote the organization of a School or of Schools of Finance and Economy among our institutions of learning, and report upon the same to the next Convention.

On motion, the report was adopted.

---

*Committee on Schools of Finance and Economy appointed by Executive Council.*

At a meeting of the Executive Council held at the close of the Convention on September 5, the foregoing resolutions were referred to the following named Committee, appointed by Mr. Charles Parsons, Chairman pro tem., as a Committee on Schools of Finance and Economy: William H. Rhawn, *Chairman*, President National Bank of the Republic, Philadelphia; George S. Coe, President American Exchange National Bank, New York; Lyman J. Gage, Vice-President First National Bank, Chicago; Morton McMichael, Cashier First National Bank, Philadelphia; and Asa P. Potter, President Maverick National Bank, Boston.

www.ingramcontent.com/pod-product-compliance
Lightning Source LLC
Chambersburg PA
CBHW021550270326
41930CB00008B/1442